CONTENTS

KU-705-913

SHIPWRECK!

'What happened?' splutters Amelie, coughing up mouthfuls of salty water and rubbing sand and seaweed off her face.

'That huge wave was too much for our boat,' replies Jess, glancing around at the scattered pieces of wood and the ripped sail. 'Zac, are you okay?'

'Well, if you call being cold, wet and stranded on a strange island in the middle of nowhere okay, then I suppose I am,' grumbles Zac. 'What's Ben doing?'

'I'm looking for my keys,' replies Ben from the water's edge. 'They're small so they'll **float**.'

'No, it's not just big things that **sink** and small things that float,' says Amelie. 'Look under the water, your keys will have sunk to the bottom.'

WHAT DO YOU THINK?

Ben thinks all small things float and all big things sink. Is he right?

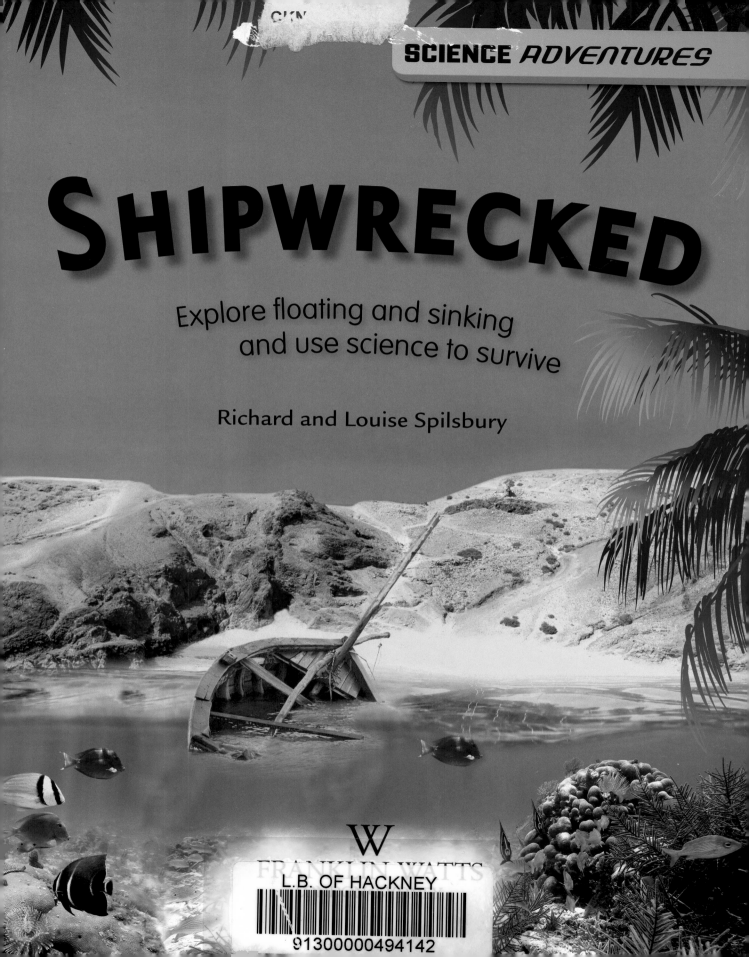

SHIPWRECKED

Explore floating and sinking
and use science to survive

Richard and Louise Spilsbury

W

FRANKLIN WATTS

First published in 2014 by
Franklin Watts
338 Euston Road
London NW1 3BH

Franklin Watts Australia
Level 17/207 Kent Street
Sydney NSW 2000

Copyright © White-Thomson Publishing Ltd 2014

Produced for Franklin Watts by
White-Thomson Publishing
+44 (0)843 208 7460
www.wtpub.co.uk

Series concept and editor: Alice Harman
Series consultant: Penny Coltman
Designer: Alix Wood
Experiment and character artworks: Stefan Chabluk

A CIP catalogue record for this book is available from
the British Library.

HB ISBN: 978 1 4451 2304 2
Library ebook ISBN: 978 1 4451 2683 8
Dewey Classification: 532.2'5

Picture Credits
Shutterstock: Andrij Vatsyk, Daniel J. Rao, Francesco Carucci,
grafikfoto, holbox, Jaco van Rensburg, kamnuan, Kees
Zwanenburg, Krofoto, My Life Graphic, Natalia Daidovich,
Ozerov Alexander, Renate Micallef, photosync, Pierre-Yves Babelon,
Potapov Alexander, Ralph Loesche, Tania Thomson, tarasov,
TTphoto, Vilainecrevette, worldswildlifewonders, xpixel, Yarygin,
Zeliko Radojko.

Every attempt has been made to clear copyright. Should there
be any inadvertent omissions, please apply to the publisher
for rectification.

Printed in China

Franklin Watts is a division of Hachette Children's Books,
an Hachette UK Company.

www.hachette.co.uk

Bold words in the text are included in the glossary

WHO'S WHO?

JESS

Jess is a bit of a daredevil. She's always first to try something new. She loves skateboarding, climbing and adventure stories.

BEN

Ben is a bit of a kit monster. He carries his rucksack with him at all times and it's full of useful – and not so useful – stuff.

AMELIE

Amelie is a science whizz. She's not a know-it-all, but she often has the right answers. She isn't too keen on getting her clothes dirty and her hair messed up.

ZAC

Zac is the youngest and although he never wants to be left out, he can get a bit nervous and is easily spooked.

PROVE IT!

Test some objects to see which float and which sink.

You need:
- big bowl
- water
- key
- small stone
- apple
- **inflated** balloon

1 Fill a big bowl with water. Predict what will happen before you put the key and the stone on the water. Now try it. Do they float or sink?

2 Predict what will happen when you put the apple and the balloon on the water. Now try it. Do they sink or float?

WHY IT WORKS

Ben is wrong. It's not just size that makes objects float or sink. You should find that keys, stones and other small but heavy objects sink, while apples, balloons and other large but lightweight objects float. How well something floats is called its **buoyancy**.

MESSAGE IN A BOTTLE

'I've got a bad feeling about this island,' says Zac. 'We don't know who or what lives here, and I keep hearing strange noises behind those trees. We need to get someone to come and rescue us, but how can we contact anyone?'

'Well, Ben found this glass bottle in his rucksack, so I'm going to put a message in it and try to float it away like they do in movies,' replies Amelie.

'That'll never work,' interrupts Jess. 'Glass bottles are heavy. It'll sink before it gets anywhere.'

'Trust me – once the lid is sealed, it'll float a long way,' says Amelie firmly.

'Just let her try it,' sighs Zac. 'Anything to help us get off this island!'

WHAT DO YOU THINK?

Amelie says a heavy, near-empty bottle can float if its lid is sealed. Is she right?

PROVE IT!

Test whether **hollow** objects float.
You need:

● big bowl or sink ● water ● lemon
● hollow, open objects such as plastic mug, glass bottle, little bowl, empty drinks can

1  Put some hollow objects in water. Do they all float? Now push them under the water. What happens?

2 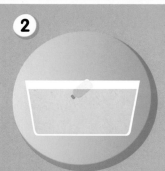 Put a small amount of water into a glass bottle, and then put on and tighten the lid. Does the bottle float or sink? How much water do you have to put inside the bottle before it sinks?

WHY IT WORKS

Hollow objects contain air. When you push unsealed hollow objects under water, the water replaces the air inside them, and we see bubbles of air come out. The **density** of an object (how heavy it is for its size) makes it float or sink. An object that contains lots of air can be light for its size, and this low density means it can float. If you seal a hollow bottle, the air stays in it and helps it to stay afloat. Even with some water inside the bottle, its density is still low enough that it will float. Water is heavier than air, so as you replace more and more of the air inside the bottle with water, the bottle eventually sinks.

WARNING:

Be very careful when using glass bottles and jars. They can easily break, and you could hurt yourself on the sharp broken glass.

LOST

'Very clever, Amelie!' snaps Jess. 'You proved hollow objects can float, but you let that bottle float away before we could put a note in it. We're lost, and now there's no way to get help!'

'It's okay,' says Zac. 'I found this hollow plastic box with a lid. We can scratch a message on a flat rock and tie it to the top of the box. As the box floats along, people will be able to read the message!'

'No, Zac, it's not just water getting inside hollow objects that can make them sink,' says Amelie. 'The water is extra weight, and that's what makes the objects sink. The added weight of that rock would mean the plastic box wouldn't float.'

WHAT DO YOU THINK?

Zac thinks that hollow objects always float. Is he right?

PROVE IT!

Find out if hollow objects always float.
You need:

● clean, empty ice-cream or margarine tub with lid
● weights, such as small stones
● big bowl ● water

1  Place one of the stones inside the tub, and put on the lid. Place the tub on the surface of a big bowl or sink of water. What happens?

2  What happens when you repeat this with all the stones inside the sealed tub? Try it several more times, taking out one stone and resealing the tub each time. What happens?

WHY IT WORKS

When an object is in water, the water pushes back up on it. This pushing force is called **upthrust**. The force that pulls an object down is called **gravity**. When these forces are balanced, objects float. Adding extra **weight** unbalances the forces until gravity is stronger than upthrust, which means the object sinks. When the extra weight is removed, the lower density of the tub makes it float up again. Zac is wrong – hollow objects do not always float.

SHARK!

'Well, I'm sorry my floating message idea didn't work, but I don't think Jess should be looking for other stuff from the wreck in that rough sea,' says Zac. 'And what's that behind her?'

'Oh no!' shouts Amelie in panic. 'Look out, Jess, there's a shark behind you! I can see its fin!'

Jess glances back and screams in horror, but then she begins to laugh. 'That's no shark. It's an upturned crate. I'll bring it in – there might be food in it!'

Jess drags the crate easily through the water, but struggles when she reaches the beach. 'I must be tired or ill,' she says. 'This crate feels so heavy now.'

?

WHAT DO YOU THINK?

Should Jess be worried that the crate feels heavier on land than it did in water?

PROVE IT!

You need:

- long elastic band ● large lump of modelling clay
- sink or big bowl ● water ● string ● scissors

Attach the lump of modelling clay to an elastic band, and hold the elastic band in the air so the clay hangs from it. Look at how much the elastic band is stretched.

1

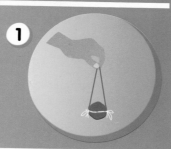

Now rest the modelling clay on the surface of a big bowl or sink of water. Again, hold the elastic band above it in the air so that the clay hangs from it. Look at how much the elastic band is stretched when the clay is in the water.

2

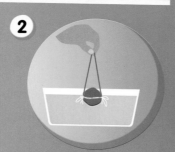

WHY IT WORKS

In air, the modelling clay stretches the elastic band more than it does when the clay is resting on water. Gravity is pulling down on the clay in air and water, but in the water upthrust force pushes up on the clay too, so it appears to weigh less. The effect stops when the clay is out of the water again. This is why Jess finds the crate so much easier to move in the water than on dry land.

'You're not getting weaker,' says Amelie. 'It's just that in the sea the upthrust force from the water pushed up on the crate, making it feel lighter.'

'That's a relief,' exclaims Jess. 'But I'm still feeling weak – with hunger. Let's open the crate!'

'I'll go and find something to prise it open,' smiles Ben. 'I know better than to keep you waiting for food!'

GONE FISHING

'After all that effort, that flippin' crate was empty! Can you hurry up and catch a fish?' whines Jess.

'I'm trying,' says Zac. 'But – argh! Something's got me, it feels like an octopus wrapping its tentacles around my ankle!'

'You're just tangled in seaweed,' says Ben calmly. 'Help me by chasing those fish this way, they're impossible to catch! How do they move up and down in the water so fast?'

'It's to do with the air they have inside them,' explains Amelie. 'Give me that ketchup sachet and drinks bottle from your rucksack and I'll prove it!

WHAT DO YOU THINK?

Is Amelie right? Do fish use air to float and sink?

PROVE IT!

Test whether air inside an object can help it move up and down in water.
You need:

- plastic drinking straw ● water
- empty and clean two-litre drink bottle
- paper clip ● modelling clay (type that can float in water)

1  Cut the plastic straw about two-thirds of the way down, then bend the short part in half. Bend the paper clip to separate its two U-shapes, and then slide one into each end of the straw.

2 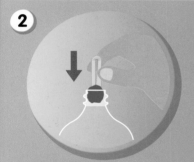 Mould a small blob of clay over the open ends of the straw. Fill the bottle with water and place your 'diver' in it. Adjust the amount of clay until the diver just floats at the top.

3  Put the lid on tightly. Holding the bottle in both hands, squeeze hard. What happens? Now release the bottle. What happens?

WHY IT WORKS

When you squeeze the bottle, water presses on the straw diver and squashes the air bubble that is inside the straw. This makes the air bubble smaller and the straw diver denser, so it sinks. When you release the pressure, the bubble expands. This makes the straw diver less dense, so it floats up. Most fish rise and sink using a part of their body called a swim bladder, which they fill or empty with air to alter their density. Amelie is right.

WE'RE NOT ALONE!

'Why are we exploring back here? It's cold and dark and I can hear a spooky banging sound,' whispers Zac.

'We have to find food and something to help us get off this island,' says Jess. 'But that noise is strange. Maybe we're not alone...'

'No, look – it's just an old boat knocking against the tree at the edge of this lake,' says Ben. 'We can use the boat to escape!'

'It's too low in the water,' says Jess, shaking her head. 'Seawater is heavier because of all the salt in it, and it will drag the boat down even more. We'll drown if we try to escape in that thing.'

'No,' says Amelie. 'It'll float better in the salty sea than on this freshwater lake.'

WHAT DO YOU THINK?

Is Amelie right? Do objects float better in salty water than in fresh water?

PROVE IT!

Test whether objects float better in salty water than in fresh water.
You need:

- two uncooked eggs (with no cracks in their shells) ● tablespoon
- two tall drinking glasses ● salt ● water

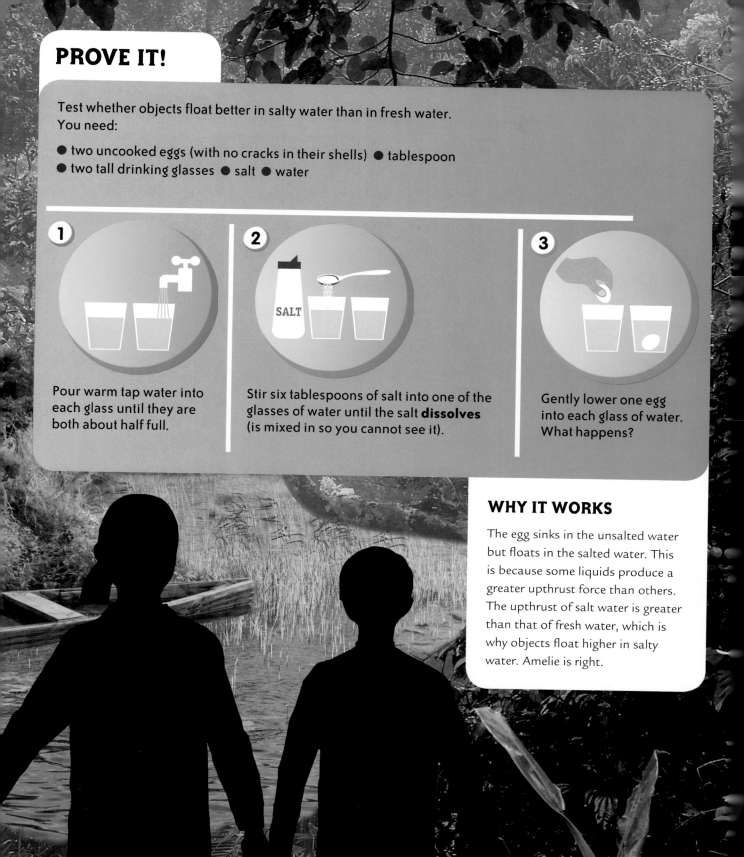

1 Pour warm tap water into each glass until they are both about half full.

2 Stir six tablespoons of salt into one of the glasses of water until the salt **dissolves** (is mixed in so you cannot see it).

3 Gently lower one egg into each glass of water. What happens?

WHY IT WORKS

The egg sinks in the unsalted water but floats in the salted water. This is because some liquids produce a greater upthrust force than others. The upthrust of salt water is greater than that of fresh water, which is why objects float higher in salty water. Amelie is right.

AN ESCAPE PLAN

'Look, I know we're all disappointed that the boat on the lake had a hole in it, but we'll be okay. We'll make our own,' says Ben reassuringly.

'With what? You haven't got a boat-making kit in that rucksack of yours!' snaps Jess sarcastically.

'No, of course not, but there must be lots of stuff washed up on the beaches,' replies Ben. 'We should go and look for bits that we can use.'

'Maybe, but what materials are we looking for – metal, wood, plastic or what?' asks Jess.

'Whichever floats best,' suggests Amelie. 'Let's test pieces of material that are the same size and find out.'

'Well, let's get on with it – a storm's brewing and we haven't made a shelter!' says Zac.

PROVE IT!

Test which materials float best.
You need:

● big bowl or a sink ● water
● pieces of different materials, such as wood, plastic, and metal, all roughly the same shape and size (such as a wooden, metal and plastic spoon of the same size)

WHAT DO YOU THINK?

Which materials do you think float best?

1 Fill the sink or bowl with water. Gather the test objects together and predict which you think will sink and which you think will float.

2 Place the objects on the water at the same time. What happens? Which materials sink and which materials float? Can you explain why?

WHY IT WORKS

Remember, objects float if the upthrust force from the water can balance their weight (the force of gravity pulling them down). You should find that materials that are lightweight for their size (i.e. that have a low density) will float better than those that are heavy for their size. But remember, the type of material that an object is made from is just one of the factors that can determine whether it will sink or float.

A NASTY FALL

'Guys, turn back, it's too rocky and dangerous along there,' pleads Zac. 'You're probably not going to find anything anyway.'

'What about that old, hollow log down there?' shouts Ben, pointing to a pile of wood washed up in a **cove** below them. 'We could escape in that.'

'I think it'd be better to make a wide raft from those flat planks,' calls Amelie. 'It'd be more buoyant.'

'Okay,' replies Ben. 'While you work out which one will be best, I'll go and check they're not too damaged to use.'

Ben starts to climb down the slippery, sea-splashed rocks. Suddenly he loses his grip and falls headfirst into the drop, his leg banging and scraping painfully against the rough, jagged sides.

'Nooo!' shout all his friends together.

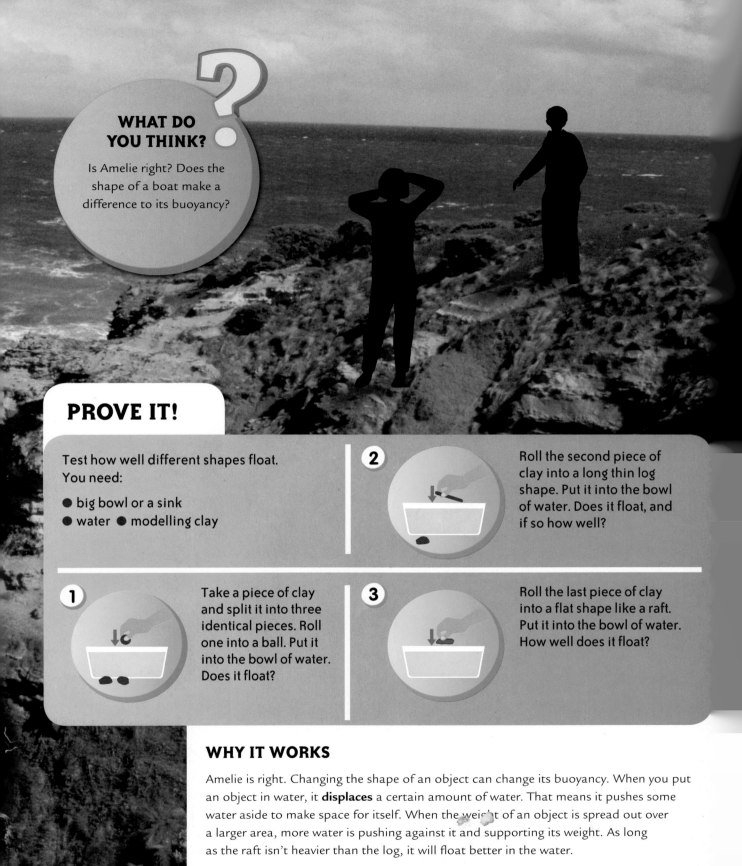

WHAT DO YOU THINK?

Is Amelie right? Does the shape of a boat make a difference to its buoyancy?

PROVE IT!

Test how well different shapes float. You need:

- big bowl or a sink
- water ● modelling clay

2 Roll the second piece of clay into a long thin log shape. Put it into the bowl of water. Does it float, and if so how well?

1 Take a piece of clay and split it into three identical pieces. Roll one into a ball. Put it into the bowl of water. Does it float?

3 Roll the last piece of clay into a flat shape like a raft. Put it into the bowl of water. How well does it float?

WHY IT WORKS

Amelie is right. Changing the shape of an object can change its buoyancy. When you put an object in water, it **displaces** a certain amount of water. That means it pushes some water aside to make space for itself. When the weight of an object is spread out over a larger area, more water is pushing against it and supporting its weight. As long as the raft isn't heavier than the log, it will float better in the water.

DANGER OF SINKING

'I don't get it. If Amelie's right, and a raft shape would float better, why aren't we making one?' asks Zac.

'We haven't got time!' barks Jess. 'Ben's leg is bleeding badly, even with the bandage that I put on it. We have to get him off this island now. Put your back into it, and let's get this hollowed-out log into the sea.'

'I'm trying, but it's heavy,' Zac snaps. 'Anyway, this thing won't fit all of us, will it? And even if we manage to cram in, it doesn't seem like it'll float with our extra weight in it.'

'You may be right, Zac,' says Amelie, sounding worried. 'The log is already low in the water. If it goes too much lower, water will get into it and we'll sink. Let's quickly test it by putting some heavy rocks in it and seeing if it floats.'

WHAT DO YOU THINK?

How can you work out how much extra weight a boat can carry and still float high enough in the water?

PROVE IT!

Make your own 'boat' and see how much weight it can carry. You need:

- clean, empty margarine or ice cream tub
- two different coloured waterproof marker pens
- set of scales ● large bowl or a sink ● water
- 250g (8oz) weight (such as a bag of dried beans)
- plastic jug or similar waterproof container

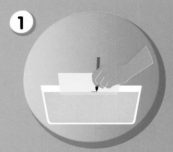

1 Float a large empty plastic tub in a large bowl or a sink full of water. Use one waterproof marker to mark where the water comes up to on the side of the tub.

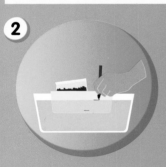

2 Load your plastic tub 'boat' with the weight. Put the weight in the middle of the tub so that the 'boat' doesn't topple over. Mark a line on the outside of the tub with a different colour marker to show where the water comes up to now.

3 Remove the weight. Place the plastic jug on the scales and weigh out 250g of water. Carefully pour this water into the tub. Mark the level of the water again on the side of the tub. What do you notice?

WHY IT WORKS

Amelie puts rocks into the hollowed-out log to test if the log still floats with added weight. When you add dried beans to your 'boat', you are adding to the weight of it. Adding weight to the tub means you increase the force of gravity on it. This changes the balance between the forces of gravity and upthrust, and the tub sinks lower in the water. When you add the 250g water, it weighs the same as the 250g bag of dried beans and so the tub sinks the same amount.

SENDING OUT AN SOS

'I know Amelie says it won't sink, but I'm not getting in that pathetic excuse for a boat,' argues Zac. 'I've been shipwrecked once today already, and I'm not risking it again!'

'You may not have to – look!' cries Jess. 'That speedboat is a long way off, but if we can attract the driver's attention we might be able to escape from this island.'

'If only we had some tissue paper to make a hot air balloon... We could write SOS on it, and then build a fire to get the hot air we need to float the balloon in the air,' says Amelie.

'Well,' says Ben, smiling. 'It just so happens that I have some tissue paper, scissors and glue in my rucksack – I forgot to take them out after my art class the other day. Let's do it!'

WHAT DO YOU THINK?

Can you use tissue paper and heat to make and fly a hot air balloon?

PROVE IT!

Try making your own hot air balloon at home. You need:

- six large sheets of tissue paper (70 x 45 cm/ 28 x 18 inches)
- strip of paper ● glue stick
- marker ● scissors ● hairdryer

2

Run the glue stick along one edge of one panel, then attach it to one edge of another panel. Press firmly to seal the two edges together, leaving a gap at the narrow end of the teardrop shape. Repeat with the other edge of each panel, glueing them to different panels in this way. Attach all six panels together to make a rounded shape.

1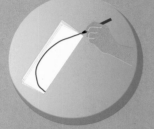

Lay the six sheets of tissue paper on top of each other and fold them in half lengthwise. Then use the marker pen to draw a half-teardrop shape that covers the whole sheet. Cut along the line and unfold the teardrop shapes. These are the panels for the hot air balloon.

3

Repair any gaps with extra glue. Then glue the strip of paper inside the opening at the narrow end of the balloon. The paper strip should fit over the hairdryer nozzle. Hold the balloon gently and put the hairdryer nozzle inside. Turn it on low, fill the balloon with hot air and watch it float!

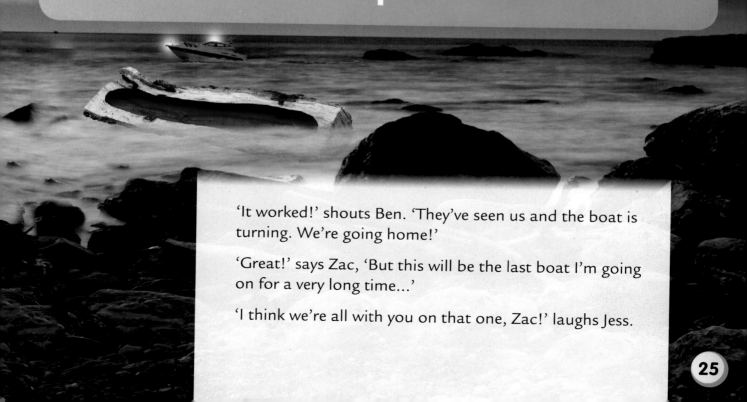

'It worked!' shouts Ben. 'They've seen us and the boat is turning. We're going home!'

'Great!' says Zac, 'But this will be the last boat I'm going on for a very long time…'

'I think we're all with you on that one, Zac!' laughs Jess.

QUIZ

1 **Which of these objects will float?**

a) coin

b) pebble

c) cork from a bottle

2 **Buoyancy means...**

a) how well something floats

b) how quickly something sinks

3 **What is density?**

a) how fast something goes

b) how light or heavy something is for its size

4 **How does a big metal boat float?**

a) Hollow objects have air inside, and that lowers their density.

b) Boats are made from a special, lightweight metal.

5 **What is the force that pushes up on things in water?**

a) gravity

b) speed

c) upthrust

6c | 7a | 8b | 9a | 10b How did you do?

6 What is the force that pulls down on things in water?

a) speed

b) upthrust

c) gravity

7 What happens when upthrust and gravity forces on an object are balanced?

a) the object floats

b) the object sinks

8 What happens when you add weight to a floating object?

a) It floats higher because adding weight increases the upthrust force.

b) It sinks lower because adding weight increases the force of gravity.

9 What happens when an object displaces water?

a) It pushes some water aside to make space for itself.

b) It soaks up some of the water around it.

10 Why does a round ball of modelling clay float if you roll it flat?

a) because flat shapes are lighter

b) because more water is pushing up against it and supporting its weight

FIND OUT MORE

BOOKS

Make It Splash! (Whizzy Science)
Anna Claybourne, Wayland, 2013

Experiments with Water: Water and Buoyancy (Do It Yourself)
Chris Oxlade, Heinemann Library, 2010

Exploring Forces (A Sense Of Science)
Claire Llewellyn, Franklin Watts, 2011

Give It a Push! Give It a Pull! A Look at Forces (Lightning Bolt Books: Exploring Physical Science)
Jennifer Boothroyd, Lerner Publications, 2010

Tabletop Scientist – The Science of Water: Projects and Experiments with Water Science and Power
Steve Parker, Dover Publications, 2013

WEBSITES

Recap the basics of floating and sinking:
www.bbc.co.uk/schools/digger/5_7entry/8.shtml

Use your knowledge to make some things float and others sink in this game:
www.wonderville.ca/asset/buoyancy-and-boats

Learn more about hot air balloons floating and sinking:
www.pbs.org/wgbh/nova/balloon/science/density

GLOSSARY

buoyancy how well something floats

cove small, sheltered bay on a coastline

density how light or heavy something is for its size

displace to make something move from its usual place

dissolve when a solid mixes into a liquid and seems to disappear

float to rest or move on (or near) the surface of water or another liquid

gravity Earth's gravity is a force that pulls objects down towards the centre of the Earth

hollow something is hollow if it has a hole or an empty space inside it

inflated filled with air or gas

material matter from which an object is or can be made

sink to move down below the surface of water or another liquid

upthrust upward force that a liquid exerts on an object that is floating in it

weight an object's weight is the force with which gravity is pulling on it

INDEX